AAT

Personal Tax
(Finance Act 2020)

For assessments from
1 January 2021 to 31 January 2022

Pocket notes

These Pocket Notes support study for the following AAT qualifications:
AAT Professional Diploma in Accounting – Level 4
AAT Level 4 Diploma in Business Skills
AAT Professional Diploma in Accounting at SCQF Level 8

British library cataloguing-in-publication data

A catalogue record for this book is available from the British Library.

Published by:
Kaplan Publishing UK
Unit 2 The Business Centre
Molly Millars Lane
Wokingham
Berkshire
RG41 2QZ

ISBN 978-1-78740-827-2

© Kaplan Financial Limited, 2020

Printed and bound in Great Britain.

CONTENTS

		Reference to Study text chapter	Page Number

Preface

These pocket notes contain the key things you need to know for the assessment, presented in a unique visual way that makes revision easy and effective.

Written by experienced lecturers and authors, these pocket notes break down content into manageable chunks to maximise your concentration.

Quality and accuracy are of the utmost importance to us so if you spot an error in any of our products, please send an email to mykaplanreporting@kaplan.com with full details, or follow the link to the feedback form in MyKaplan.

Our Quality Co-ordinator will work with our technical team to verify the error and take action to ensure it is corrected in future editions.

A guide to the assessment

- The assessment.
- The keys to success in AAT personal tax.
- Guidance from the chief assessor.

The assessment

Personal tax is an optional unit on the Professional Diploma in Accounting qualification.

Personal tax is assessed by means of a computer based assessment. The CBA will last for 2 hours 30 minutes and consist of 13 tasks.

In any one assessment, students may not be assessed on all content, or on the full depth or breadth of a piece of content. The content assessed may change over time to ensure validity of assessment, but all assessment criteria will be tested over time.

Learning outcomes and weighting

1	Analyse the theories, principles and rules that underpin taxation systems	10%
2	Calculate a UK taxpayer's total income	28%
3	Calculate income tax and National Insurance (NI) contributions payable by a UK taxpayer	23%
4	Account for capital gains tax	27%
5	Discuss the basics of inheritance tax	12%
	Total	100%

Pass mark

To pass a unit assessment, students need to achieve a mark of 70% or more.

This unit contributes 10% of the total amount required for the Professional Diploma in Accounting qualification.

Sample assessment

The tasks in the sample assessment test the following areas.

1   Professional conduct in relation to taxation
2   Employment income benefits – provision of cars
3   Employment income benefits – other benefits
4   Investment income
5   Income from property
6   Calculation of income tax liability
7   National insurance contributions
8   Minimising tax
9   Knowledge of capital gains tax
10 Chargeable gain on a disposal of shares
11 Calculation of capital gains tax
12 Knowledge of inheritance tax
13 Calculation of inheritance tax

Format of objective questions

The standard task formats that will be used for any computer based assessment are as follows:

- True or False (tick boxes).
- Multiple choice, with anything from three to six options available.
- Gap fill, using either words or numbers.
- Pick lists, or drop down options, which are quite likely for tax returns.
- Drag and drop, which can only be used if the question and the possible answers can fit on one screen.
- Hybrids, a mixture of the above.

The keys to success in AAT personal tax

- Attempt all of the tasks.
- Learn the computational pro formas. This will enable you to adopt a structured approach to a question.
- Practise questions to improve your ability to apply the techniques and perform the calculations.

Guidance from the chief assessor

You should read each task carefully before attempting to answer it.

Make sure you scroll down to the bottom of each page before moving on to the next question. Students often miss parts of questions.

When carrying out extended written tasks:

- Follow the 'Guidance on extended writing tasks' — prepared by the chief assessor. This can be found on the AAT website and is included in the Kaplan study text in Chapter 1.

1

Introduction to personal tax

- Tax planning, tax avoidance and tax evasion.
- Duties and responsibilities.
- Professional conduct in relation to taxation.
- Taxation of individuals.
- Tax year.
- Residence.
- Domicile.

Tax planning, tax avoidance and tax evasion

- Tax planning is using the tax system as intended to minimise tax.
- Tax avoidance is legal, but not following the intent of the law.
- Tax evasion is dishonestly withholding or falsifying information: it is illegal.

Duties and responsibilities

- An AAT tax adviser has duties and responsibilities to:
  - the client
  - HM Revenue & Customs
  - AAT.
- AAT's Code of Professional Ethics sets out its expectations of members (EPOS):

Ethical approach	Adopt an ethical approach to work, employers and clients.
Professional duty	Acknowledge a professional duty to society as a whole.
Objective	Be objective.
Standards	Provide professional, high standards of service, conduct and performance at all times.

Professional conduct in relation to taxation

Extracts relating to professional conduct are available for you to refer to in the assessment.

Main areas:

- Fundamental principles
- Tax returns
- Tax advice
- Irregularities
- Access to data by HMRC

You must know your way around the document

Confidentiality

- A tax adviser has an overriding duty of confidentiality towards his client.
- No information should be disclosed to a third party without the client's consent.

- Whilst acting in the client's best interest, the tax adviser must deal with HMRC in an open and constructive manner.
- Duty of confidentiality only overridden where there is a legal, regulatory or professional duty to disclose (e.g. where money laundering is suspected).

Money laundering

Exchange of funds acquired through crime for funds that do not appear to be linked to crime.

Accountants should:

- check identity of prospective clients
- appoint a Money Laundering Reporting Officer (MLRO)
- report any suspected money laundering to MLRO.

Tax advice and records

- In providing tax advice and preparing tax returns a tax adviser must:
  - Act in the best interests of the client.
  - Ensure services comply with the law and are carried out competently.
- Advice must not be given or associated with any communication that is believed to be false or misleading.

Errors and omissions

- Advise client of implications.
- Cease to act unless HMRC notified.
- Inform HMRC but do not give reasons.

Taxation of individuals

The main taxes applied to individuals are

Income tax

Charged on:

- taxable income
- in the tax year.

Capital gains tax

Charged on:

- taxable gains
- in the tax year.

National insurance

Charged on:

- earnings of employee
- in the tax year.

Inheritance tax

Charged on:

- transfers of value
- in the tax year.

Tax year

- Also known as:
  - year of assessment
- Runs from 6 April to following 5 April.

CBA focus

Tax year 2020/21.

6 April 2020 to 5 April 2021.

Residence

- UK residents are taxed on UK and overseas income.
- Non-UK residents are taxed on UK income only.

Determination of status

Three steps (consider in this order):

1. Satisfy an automatic non-UK resident test = non-UK resident
2. Satisfy an automatic UK resident test = UK resident
3. Consider days in the UK and number of UK ties.

Automatic non-UK resident test

- in UK for less than 16 days, or

- in UK for less than 46 days and not resident in three previous years, or

- in UK for less than 91 days and work full-time overseas.

Automatic UK resident test

- in UK for at least 183 days, or

- only home in UK, or

- work full-time in the UK.

Sufficient ties tests

- Close family in the UK
- A house in the UK made use of during the tax year
- Substantive work in the UK
- 90 days + in the UK in either/both of previous two tax years
- More time in UK than any other country in the tax year

The number of ties required depends on the number of days spent in the UK and whether the individual was resident in the UK in the previous three tax years.

Domicile

- Acquire father's domicile at birth.
- Can acquire new domicile at age 16.
  - Sever all ties with UK and move abroad permanently.

Deemed domicile

- Condition A = domicile of origin in the UK + acquired non-UK domicile of choice + UK resident in at least one of the two previous tax years
- Condition B = resident in the UK for 15 of the previous 20 tax years

2

Principles of income tax

- Principles of income tax.
- Taxable income.
- Exempt income.
- Pro forma – Income tax computation.

One of the tasks in the assessment may involve calculating what income is taxable for an individual or calculation of an individual's income tax payable.

It is essential to understand and learn the layout of the income tax computation.

Principles of income tax

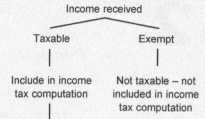

Taxable income

Taxed at different income tax rates depending on type of income.

Non-savings	Savings	Dividends
↓	↓	↓
Employment income	Interest	Dividends received
Trading profits		
Property income		

- Income must be included gross.

- Trading profits and property income are received gross.

- Employment income is received net of PAYE, but is quoted gross in questions.

Exempt income

- Income from Individual Savings Accounts (ISAs).

- Interest on NS&I Savings Certificates.

- Gambling/lottery winnings/prizes.

- Statutory redundancy pay.

- Interest on delayed income tax repayments.

- Some social security benefits.

- Interest on Save As You Earn (SAYE) sharesave accounts.

- Scholarships/educational grants.

- Damages for personal injury or death.

Pro forma – Income tax computation

	Non-savings £	Savings £	Dividends £	Total £
Employment income	X			X
Trading profits	X			X
Property income	X			X
Interest income		X		X
Dividends received			X	X
Net income	X	X	X	X
Less: Personal allowance	(X)			(X)
Taxable income	X	X	X	X
Income tax	@ 20/40/45%			X
		@ 0/20/40/45%		X
			@ 0/7.5/32.5/38.1%	X
Income tax liability				X
Less: Tax deducted at source				(X)
Income tax payable				X

CBA focus

It is essential to understand and learn the layout of the income tax computation.

Task 6 of the sample assessment requires the computation of income tax payable.

In your assessment you may not be able to enter a full computation. See Chapter 7 for further details.

3

Introduction to employment income

- Introduction.
- Employment v self-employment.
- Basis of assessment.
- Allowable deductions.

CBA focus

Employment income is a key topic which is highly likely to be examined in the assessment.

Key Point

Employment income covers all earnings received from an employment.

Earnings include salaries, wages, directors' fees, bonuses, commissions, expense allowances, tips, benefits.

Introduction

Pro forma – Employment income

	£
Salary/wages/bonuses	X
Expenses reimbursed (1)	X
Benefits (see Chapter 4)	X
	X
Less: Allowable deductions	
Employee pension contributions (2)	(X)
Professional subscriptions	(X)
Give as you earn (3)	(X)
Business travel	(X)
Other allowable expenses	(X)
Taxable employment income	X

Notes:

(1) Unless in relation to tax allowable expenses incurred by employee.

(2) To occupational pension scheme.

(3) Charitable donations via an approved payroll giving scheme.

Employment v self-employment

An employee works under a **contract of service** and a self-employed person under a **contract for services**.

The main criteria to look at when deciding between the two are:

- control
- financial risk
- equipment – who provides
- work performance and correction
- holidays and sickness benefits
- exclusivity.

Basis of assessment

- Employment income is taxed in the tax year in which the income is received.
- Earlier of:
  - date of receipt
  - date employee becomes entitled to receipt.

Allowable deductions

General rule

Expenses must be incurred wholly, exclusively and necessarily in the performance of the duties of employment.

Other specifically allowable deductions

Pension contributions	By an employee to a company's occupational pension scheme (see Chapter 8)
Professional subscriptions	e.g. AAT, trade associations
Payroll giving/GAYE	Charitable donations deducted from salary under an approved payroll giving scheme

Entertaining

Customer entertaining

Allowable if:	Not allowable if:
↓	↓
Met from specific entertaining allowance	Met from general expense allowance

Business travel

- Business travel is travel made in the performance of an employee's duties (e.g. travel to client meetings).
- Travel between home and the normal place of work is not business travel.

Approved Mileage Allowance Payments (AMAP)

Applies where an employee is paid a mileage rate by the employer for using his own car for business travel.

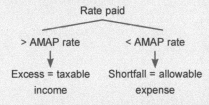

Rate paid

> AMAP rate	< AMAP rate
↓	↓
Excess = taxable income	Shortfall = allowable expense

CBA focus

The AMAP rates are provided in the taxation tables available in the assessment.

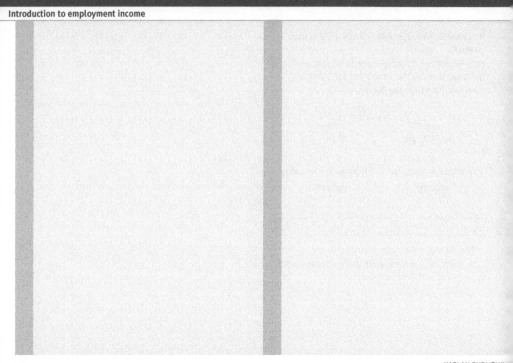

4

Employment income – benefits

- Exempt benefits.
- General principles.
- Living accommodation.
- Job related accommodation.
- Company cars.
- Fuel benefit.
- Company vans.
- Beneficial loans.
- Use of assets.
- Gift/purchase of assets.

CBA focus

Employment benefits are tested in tasks 2 and 3 of the sample assessment.

You need to understand the general principles and the special computational rules for each of the commonly provided benefits.

Exempt benefits

- Job related accommodation.
- Subsidised canteen (if available to all staff).
- Removal expenses (up to £8,000).
- Parking space (at or near workplace).
- One mobile phone per employee.
- Workplace nurseries.
- Employer contributions of up to £6 per week for additional household costs for employees working from home.
- Employer's pension contributions (Chapter 8).
- Workplace sports and recreational facilities.
- Work-related training.
- Trivial benefits <£50 per gift.
- Entertainment, such as a staff Christmas party (up to £150 per attendee per tax year).

- Long service awards (£50 for each year of service maximum 20 years).
- Personal expenses incurred when working away on company business (up to £5 per night).
- Bicycles or cycling safety equipment (if available to all staff).
- Eye tests and/or corrective glasses for VDU users.
- Awards from staff suggestion scheme.
- Gifts from someone other than employer costing no more than £250 per tax year.
- Annual private medical and/or health screening.
- Occasional provision of night taxi.
- Subsidised work buses.
- Scholarships (many rules).
- Pay whilst attending a full time course - £15,480.

General principles

When calculating the taxable amount for any benefit consider:

Key Point

- Payments made by the employee for the benefit.
- Time apportionment when the benefit is only available for part of the tax year.

	£
Benefit calculated for tax year	X
Periods where unavailable	(X)
Employee contributions	(X)*
Taxable benefit	X

* except partial contributions towards the cost of private fuel

Taxable benefits

Benefit	Amount taxable
General rule	Cost to employer
Cash vouchers	Cash for which voucher can be exchanged
Non cash vouchers	Cost to employer
Credit cards	All items purchased for personal use (not interest or card charges)
Living accommodation	Up to three components (see below)
Cars & fuel	Based on CO_2 emissions
Vans & fuel	Based on a scale charge

Benefit	Amount taxable
Interest free/low interest loans	Based on official rate of interest
Use of assets	Based on 20% of market value of asset
Gift of new asset	Cost to employer
Gift of asset after use	Greater of (1) Market value when gifted (2) Market value when first used less amounts already taxed
Other	Marginal cost to the employer

Living accommodation

Benefit	Amount taxable
Basic charge	Higher of: – Annual value – Rent paid by employer
Expensive accommodation charge	Where the cost of the property is >£75,000. (Cost – £75,000) x official rate of interest (will be provided in the assessment)

If property is over 6 years old at the time it is provided to employee then replace 'Cost' with market value at date accommodation made available.

Key Point

Where the employer rents rather than owns the accommodation there can never be an expensive accommodation charge.

Ancillary benefits	Amount taxable
Use of furniture	20% x market value when first provided
Living expenses e.g. heating, electricity, decorating	Cost to employer

Job related accommodation

Definition

Accommodation which is:

- Necessary for proper performance of employee's duties, or
- Provided for the better performance of duties and it is customary to provide such accommodation, or
- Provided as part of special security arrangements because of a specific threat to the employee's security.

- Consequences:

Benefit	Amount taxable
Basic charge	Exempt
Expensive accommodation charge	Exempt
Ancillary benefits	As for non-job related accommodation except: Maximum benefit restricted to 10% of other employment income

Company cars

- Benefit arises where an employer provides a car and it is available for private use.
- Benefit:

Relevant %   x   **List price of car (when new)**

- Based on CO_2 emissions (g/km)
- 14% + 1% for every 5g/km over 55g/km
- Additional 2% for cars registered pre 6 April 2020 (except pure electric vehicles)
- 4% diesel supplement
- 37% overall cap

- Include extras (over £100)
- Reduced by employee capital contribution (max £5,000)
- Additional 2% for cars registered pre 6 April 2020 (except pure electric vehicles)

Relevant percentages for low emission cars

CO_2 emissions for petrol engines in g/km	Electric range in miles	%
Nil		0
1 to 50	≥130	0
1 to 50	70-129	3
1 to 50	40-69	6
1 to 50	30-39	10
1 to 50	<30	12
51 to 54		13

- Lower % for cars with very low emissions (see table) - 4% diesel supplement also applies here.

- The 4% diesel supplement does not apply to diesel cars which meet RDE2 standards.

- Car unavailable for part of the year:
  - Proportional reduction in benefit only if car unavailable for ≥ 30 days.
- Employee contributions for private use:
  - reduce taxable benefit.
- Cars only used for business (e.g. pool cars) – no taxable benefit.
- Car benefit figure includes all running costs of the car (i.e. there is no additional benefit for insurance, services, etc.) paid for by the employer.

Fuel benefit

- Where fuel is provided for private use of a company car
- Benefit

  Relevant car %   x   £24,500

- No benefit if:
  - Employee pays for all fuel for private use
  - Fuel is only provided for business use
- If private fuel is permanently withdrawn or car unavailable for ≥ 30 days the benefit is proportionately reduced.

Company vans

Taxed on a scale charge.

- Zero emission vans – 80% of scale charge
- Other vans – £3,490
- Private fuel – £666 (£nil if the van has zero emissions).
- Time apportion if not available for part of year.
- No benefit if private use is insignificant or limited to ordinary commuting between home and work.

Beneficial loans

Taxable benefit where an employee is provided with an interest free or cheap loan:

	£
Loan outstanding at official rate of interest (ORI)	X
Less: Interest paid by employee	(X)
Taxable benefit	X

- No benefit if:
  - Total of loans outstanding throughout the year is < £10,000, or
  - Loan is used to:
    - purchase equipment for employment, or
    - pay for allowable employment expenses.
- Two methods of calculating benefit:
  - Average method.
  - Precise method – interest calculated on a daily basis.

Average method £
½ (balance at start of year +
balance at end of year) x ORI X
Less: Interest paid by employee (X)
                                  X

Loan provided in year £
½ (balance at start of loan +
balance at end of year) x X/12 x ORI X
Less: Interest paid by employee (X)
                                  X

Loan fully repaid in year £
½ (balance at start of year +
balance when repaid)
x X/12 x ORI X
Less: Interest paid by employee (X)
                                  X

Where X = no. of months loan outstanding in
tax year
Note: In assessment interest paid by employee
should be calculated on average basis.

Use of assets

Where an employee is allowed to use an
asset for private purposes the taxable benefit
is:

20% x Market value of asset when first
        provided to any employee.

Gift/purchase of assets

A benefit arises where an asset is gifted to an employee or is purchased from the employer.

The taxable benefit depends on whether the asset is new or previously used by an employee:

Asset	Benefit	
New	Cost to the company less price paid by employee	
Used	Higher of:	£
	(1) MV at date of gift/purchase	X
	Less: Price paid	
	by employee	(X)
		X
	(2) MV when first provided	X
	Less: Benefits already	
	taxed	(X)
	Less: Price paid	
	by employee	(X)
		X

This rule does not apply to cars or bicycles; use computation (1) only for these.

5

Property income

- Taxable property income.
- Allowable expenditure.
- Capital expenditure.
- Motor expenses.
- Property losses.
- Property allowance.

Property income is very likely to be examined in the assessment.

You need to be able to compute the taxable profit or allowable loss arising from the letting of property.

Property income is tested in task 5 of the sample assessment.

Taxable property income

Tax is normally charged on income and expenses **actually received or paid** in the tax year = **cash basis**.

The taxpayer can elect to be assessed on the rent due less the expenses payable for the tax year = **accruals basis**.

The accruals basis is automatically used if gross annual rents > £150,000.

Where an individual has more than one rental property, the same basis must be used for all properties. Rental income and expenditure is pooled, on the appropriate basis, to calculate the taxable property income on all properties for a tax year:

	£
Rental income	X
Less: Allowable expenses	(X)
Taxable property income	X

Chapter 5

Allowable expenditure

Expenses must be incurred 'wholly and exclusively' for the purposes of the letting.

Examples

- Repairs & maintenance
- Redecoration
- Cleaning/gardening
- Council tax
- Water rates
- Advertising
- Insurance
- Agent's commission

- Interest on loan to acquire/improve the property (non-residential properties only in PLTX)
- Professional and legal fees (e.g. tenancy agreements, accounts, collecting rents)

Note:

Private use of property by the owner means expenses which do not relate to lettings must be time apportioned.

Capital expenditure

Cash basis

Capital expenditure is generally allowable when it is incurred, except for new capital items used in residential property lets.

The cost of replacing domestic items is allowable:

- deduction is restricted to cost of similar item
- less any proceeds from original asset.

Accruals basis

Capital expenditure is generally disallowed (e.g. property improvements).

Capital expenditure on the initial purchase of furniture is disallowed, but replacements are allowed on the same basis as above.

Motor expenses

A landlord can claim a deduction for business mileage using the approved mileage allowance payments (AMAP) rates as in chapter 3.

Property losses

- A property loss is calculated in exactly the same way as a profit
- Where a loss on property arises in a tax year:
    - The property income for the year is £Nil.
    - The loss is carried forward and relieved against the next available profits from property letting.

Key Point

Where there is a property loss the property income for the year is £Nil.

Never show a negative figure.

Property allowance

The property allowance is £1,000.

It can be deducted from gross rental income instead of deducting expenses.

If property income < £1,000:

- The property allowance will automatically apply and property income will be nil.
- The taxpayer will not have to declare the income.
- The taxpayer can elect for the allowance not to apply, and instead deduct expenses (e.g. to realise a loss).

If property income > £1,000:

- The taxpayer can elect to deduct the allowance instead of the allowable expenses.
- The property allowance should be claimed where expenses are less than £1,000.

6

Investment income

- Investment income.
- Types of savings income.
- Individual savings accounts (ISAs).
- Dividend income.

Task 4 of the sample assessment tests investment income.

You need to understand the tax implications of owning a variety of investments.

Investment income

- The two main types of investment income are:
  - Savings income
  - Dividend income

Investment income taxed at 0%

- Savings allowance
  - Savings income taxed at 0%.
  - Basic rate taxpayer   £1,000
  - Higher rate taxpayer   £500
- Dividend allowance
  - £2,000 of dividend income taxed at 0% for all taxpayers.

See Chapter 7 for more detail on the taxation of investment income.

Chapter 6

Types of savings income

Exempt	Taxable
Interest on: • ISAs • NS&I Savings Certificates • Delayed income tax repayments • SAYE sharesave accounts	• Bank and Building Society accounts • Gilts • NS&I accounts and bonds • Quoted loan notes (debentures) of companies

Individual savings accounts (ISAs)

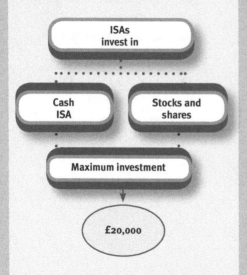

- Cash only ISAs can be opened by any UK resident aged at least 16.
- Stocks and shares ISAs can be opened by those aged 18 or more.

Dividend income

Exempt	From shares in an ISA
Taxable	All other dividends

7

Income tax payable

- Pro forma – income tax payable.
- Personal allowance.
- Tax rates.
- Calculating income tax payable.

CBA focus

- The calculation of income tax payable is tested in task 6 of the sample assessment.
- It is essential that you learn and understand the income tax payable pro forma.
- However in the CBA you will only have a limited space to enter a personal tax computation.

Pro forma – income tax payable

CBA focus

Use the pro forma to ensure that income tax is calculated at the correct rates on different sources of income.

Pro forma – Income tax computation – 2020/21

	Non-savings £	Savings £	Dividends £	Total £
Employment income	X			X
Trading profits	X			X
Property income	X			X
Interest income		X		X
Dividend income			X	X
Net income	X	X	X	X
Less: Personal Allowance	(X)			(X)
Taxable income	X	X	X	X
Income tax	@ 20/40/45%			X
		@ 0/20/40/45%		X
			@ 0/7.5/32.5/38.1%	X
Income tax liability				X
Less: PAYE				(X)
Income tax payable				X

Personal allowance

- Available to all individuals (£12,500 for 2020/21)
- Deducted from net income to give taxable income
- Not transferable
- Cannot be offset against capital gains
- Lost if not used in the year.

Restricted personal allowance

- Allowance reduced where adjusted net income exceeds £100,000.
- Reduction= 50% x (Adjusted net income – £100,000).
- No personal allowance is awarded where adjusted net income exceeds £125,000

Tax rates

Different tax rates apply depending on the amount and type of income.

	Non-savings	Savings	Dividends
Basic rate band (first £37,500)	20%	20%	7.5%
Higher rate (next £112,500)	40%	40%	32.5%
Additional rate (over £150,000)	45%	45%	38.1%

Order of calculation

(1) Non-savings income

(2) Savings income

(3) Dividends.

Details of the tax rates and bands and the personal allowance will be provided in the assessment.

Investment income taxed at 0%

- Savings allowance
    - Savings income taxed at 0%.
    - Basic rate taxpayer   £1,000
    - Higher rate taxpayer   £500
- Dividend allowance
    - £2,000 of dividend income taxed at 0% for all taxpayers.

Calculating income tax payable

- Income tax **liability** is the total amount of income tax due to HMRC in a tax year.
- Income tax **payable** is the amount outstanding after the deduction of tax already suffered at source.

	£
Income tax liability	X
Less: Tax deducted at source:	
PAYE	(X)
Income tax payable	X

CBA focus

It is important to be able to distinguish between income tax **liability** and income tax **payable**.

Approach to computations in the assessment

- Based on the sample CBA the space available for the personal income tax computation is likely to be a 3 column grid.
- Draw up your full computation on the paper provided in your assessment and check how many lines and columns are available in the answer grid to see whether you need to abbreviate your answer.
- Include simple workings.
- Likely to be a manually marked question.
- No need to enter lines marking totals and sub-totals.

8

Pensions

- Types of pension schemes.
- Tax relief.
- Mechanisms for giving tax relief.
- Pension contributions and the personal allowance.

Pension contributions are likely to feature in the assessment.

You should be aware of the tax treatment of both employer's and employee's contributions to both occupational pension schemes and personal pension schemes.

Types of pension schemes

Set up by employer. Employer usually contributes. Employee may contribute.

Self-employed, or employed but no occupational scheme available, or choose instead of (or as well as) an occupational scheme.

Chapter 8

Tax relief

- Tax relief available for pension contributions is the same for all registered pension schemes (i.e. occupational pension schemes and personal pension schemes).
- Employer contributions
  - Exempt benefit for employee.
- Individual's contributions
  - Maximum annual contributions on which an individual will obtain tax relief is:

    Higher of:

    (i) £3,600
    (ii) 100% of UK relevant earnings.

Mechanisms for giving tax relief

Tax relief for employee contributions given by:

Net pay arrangements	Deduction at source
Occupational pensions	Personal pensions
Employee contribution deducted from gross pay	Contributions are paid net of basic rate tax
	Gross contribution = (amount paid x 100/80)
Tax relief, at all rates, given through the PAYE system	Higher and additional rate tax relief is given by extending the basic rate and higher rate bands

Pension contributions and the personal allowance

- The personal allowance is restricted if adjusted net income (ANI) >£100,000
- When calculating ANI gross personal pension scheme contributions should be deducted from net income
- The ANI figure should not appear on the face of the taxable income computation but as a working for the personal allowance only

chapter

9

Charitable donations

- Types of charitable donation.
- Tax relief.
- Gift aid and personal allowances.

CBA focus

You may be required to deal with an income tax computation involving a charitable donation. Alternatively, you could have a multiple choice or true/false question testing your understanding of the tax implications of donations.

Types of charitable donation

Charitable donations

Payroll giving schemes

- Donate through payroll
- Allowable deduction from employment income

Gift aid donations

- Complete a gift aid declaration.
- Donation deemed to be net of 20% tax

Chapter 9

Tax relief

- **Payroll giving schemes**
  - Payments are made gross
  - Donation deducted from taxable employment income.
  - Tax relief given through PAYE system.
- **Gift aid donations**
  - Payment treated as made net of basic rate tax (20%). Charity recovers the basic rate tax from HMRC.
  - Higher and additional rate tax relief given to the taxpayer by extending the basic and higher rate bands in the income tax computation.

Key Point

If an individual is a basic rate taxpayer a gift aid donation has no effect on his income tax computation.

Gift aid and personal allowances

- The personal allowance is restricted if adjusted net income (ANI) >£100,000
- When calculating ANI gross gift aid donations should be deducted from net income
- The ANI figure should not appear on the face of the taxable income computation but as a working for the personal allowance only

10

National insurance contributions

- Classes of national insurance contributions (NICs).
- Employees.
- Employers.

CBA focus

National insurance contributions are tested in task 7 of the sample assessment.

Classes of national insurance contributions (NICs)

- Different classes of NICs are paid depending on the individual's status.

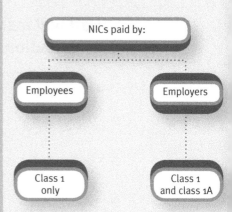

Employees

Class 1 employee's NICs

- Employees pay class 1 employee's NICs on their 'cash earnings'.
- Cash earnings includes:
  - any remuneration derived from employment and paid in money
  - vouchers exchangeable for cash or goods
  - reimbursement of cost of travel between home and work.
- Cash earnings does not include:
  - exempt employment benefits
  - most non-cash benefits
  - reimbursement of business expenses.
  - mileage allowance < 45p per mile.
- Payable by all employees
  - aged 16 to state pension age
  - Note: an upper age limit applies.

- Payable at 12% on earnings between £9,500 and £50,000.
  - Note: an upper limit applies to the 12% rate.
- Payable at 2% on earnings above £50,000.
- Contributions are collected by the employer through the PAYE scheme.
- If earnings are given on a monthly or weekly basis the annual limits must be divided by 12 or 52 as appropriate.

Employers

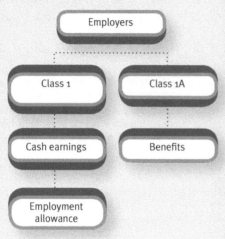

Class 1 employer's NICs

- Cost borne by employer.
- Allowable trading expense for tax purposes.
- Rate of 13.8% on earnings over £8,788 per annum.
  - Note: no upper limit.
- Paid on 'cash earnings', as for employee's class 1 NICs.
- Paid in respect of employees aged ≥ 16.
  - Note: no upper limit.
- Employment allowance available.
- Payable with employee's class 1 contributions through PAYE system.
- If earnings are given on a monthly or weekly basis the annual limits must be divided by 12 or 52 as appropriate.

Employment allowance

- Up to £4,000 per employer per year.
- Deducted from class 1 employer's NICs only.
- The employment allowance is not available to employers with total class 1 employer's NIC > £100,000 in the previous tax year (assume NICs were less than the limit if only one or two employees).

Class 1A

- Payable by the employer only.
- Rate of 13.8% on taxable benefits provided to the employee.

11

Capital gains tax – introduction

- Chargeable gains.
- Capital gains tax computation.
- Capital losses.

You should be able to calculate the capital gain/loss arising on the disposal of a variety of assets and calculate the capital gains tax payable for a tax year, applying the various reliefs and exemptions.

It is essential to learn and understand the capital gains tax computation pro forma.

Task 9 of the sample assessment covers the basics of CGT.

Chargeable gains

- A chargeable gain arises
  - when a chargeable disposal
  - is made by a chargeable person
  - of a chargeable asset.

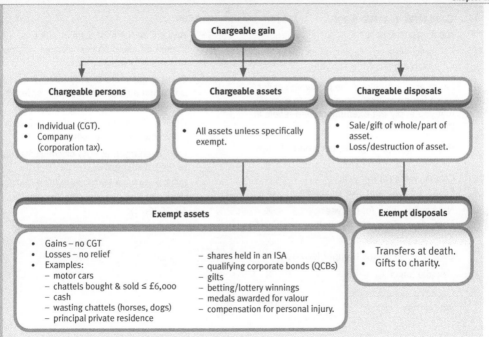

Chapter 11

Chargeable gain

Chargeable persons

- Individual (CGT).
- Company (corporation tax).

Chargeable assets

- All assets unless specifically exempt.

Chargeable disposals

- Sale/gift of whole/part of asset.
- Loss/destruction of asset.

Exempt assets

- Gains – no CGT
- Losses – no relief
- Examples:
  - motor cars
  - chattels bought & sold ≤ £6,000
  - cash
  - wasting chattels (horses, dogs)
  - principal private residence
  - shares held in an ISA
  - qualifying corporate bonds (QCBs)
  - gilts
  - betting/lottery winnings
  - medals awarded for valour
  - compensation for personal injury.

Exempt disposals

- Transfers at death.
- Gifts to charity.

Capital gains tax computation

- Individuals pay capital gains tax on their taxable gains for a tax year.

Learn and understand the following capital gains tax computation pro forma to ensure that you apply the exemptions and reliefs in the correct order.

Pro forma capital gains tax computation

	£
Capital gains for the year	X
Less: Current year capital losses	(X)
Net capital gains for the year	X
Less: Annual exempt amount	(12,300)
	X
Less: Capital losses brought forward	(X)
Taxable gains	X
Capital gains tax at the appropriate rates	X

Notes:

- Any unused annual exempt amount cannot be offset against taxable income or carried forward or back.
- Taxable gains are treated as an additional amount of income in order to determine the rate of CGT.
- CGT is charged at 10% on gains falling within the basic rate band.
- CGT is charged at 20% on the remainder of the taxable gains.
- CGT is payable by 31 January following the end of the tax year (31 January 2022 for 2020/21).

Capital losses

- Capital losses are offset against capital gains.

Current year losses	Brought forward losses
Must be set off against current year capital gains	Offset restricted to amount needed to reduce taxable gains down to nil after deducting the annual exempt amount
Offset before brought forward losses	

12

Capital gains tax – calculation of gains and losses

- Capital gains computation.
- Part disposals.
- Assets lost or destroyed.
- Assets damaged.
- Chattels.
- Connected persons.

Learn the pro forma for calculating individual gains, which applies for all disposals.

The pro forma will remind you how to compute a gain and help you present a structured answer in the real assessment.

You should also know the special rules which apply in certain circumstances (e.g. part disposals, chattel rules).

Task 9 of the sample assessment covers the basics of CGT.

Capital gains computation

	Notes	£
Gross sale proceeds	(1)	X
Less: Selling costs	(2)	(X)
Net sales proceeds		X
Less: Allowable costs	(3)	(X)
Capital gain		X

Notes:

(1) Use market value where transaction not at arm's length (e.g. gift or disposal to a connected person).

(2) Include legal fees, advertising costs etc.

(3) Include purchase price and purchase expenses (e.g. legal fees) and enhancements. Revenue expenses such as repairs are not included.

Chapter 12

Part disposals

- When part of an asset is sold, need to determine the cost of the part sold.

Formula

Cost of part of asset disposed of

= Allowable cost of whole asset x $\dfrac{A}{A + B}$

Where:

A = Proceeds of part sold

B = Market value of the remaining part

Assets lost or destroyed

- Proceeds will be any insurance or damages received.
- If there is no insurance the proceeds will be nil and a loss will arise.
- If the asset is replaced within 12 months the taxpayer can claim that no gain or loss will arise.

Assets damaged

- If there is no insurance / damages there is no disposal.
- If insurance is received there is a part disposal – use the A/A + B formula above, where:

  A = Compensation received

  B = Market value of asset in its damaged condition

- If insurance is received and used to restore asset taxpayer can claim to deduct the compensation from the cost of the asset rather than be treated as having made a part disposal.

Chattels

Chattel: Tangible moveable property (e.g. painting, dog, antique table)

Wasting Chattel: expected life ≤ 50 years (e.g. dog)

Non-wasting Chattel: expected life > 50 years (e.g. antique table, painting)

CBA focus

There will usually be a question on chattels in the assessment.

Key Point

Wasting chattels are exempt assets.

- Special rules apply to non-wasting chattels:

Sales proceeds \ Cost	£6,000 or less	More than £6,000
£6,000 or less	Exempt	Allowable loss based on deemed gross sales proceeds of £6,000
More than £6,000	Normal computation but gain is restricted to: 5/3 x (gross proceeds – £6,000)	Normal gain or loss computation

Connected persons

- Use market value instead of actual proceeds.
- If a loss arises on a disposal to a connected person it can only be offset against gains arising on disposals to the **same** connected person.

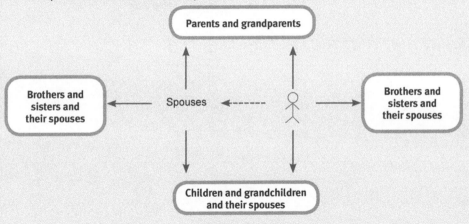

Civil partners and their relatives (as above) are also connected persons.

CBA focus

There will often be a question on connected persons in the assessment.

Transfers between spouses

- Disposals between spouses are on a no gain/no loss basis.
- Civil partnership disposals are treated in same way.

Capital gains tax – shares and securities

- Introduction.
- Matching rules.
- The share pool.
- Bonus issues.
- Rights issues.

The disposal of shares and securities is tested in task 10 of the sample assessment.

It is essential that you learn the special matching rules.

Questions involving the share pool with bonus and rights issues are common. Matching rules are often tested.

Introduction

- Where shares of the same type in a company have been acquired through more than one purchase, rules are needed to identify which shares have been disposed of.

Matching rules

- Shares of the same type are matched as follows:

    - Same day acquisitions.

    - Acquisitions in the 30 days after disposal.

    - Acquisitions in share pool.

- The cost is used in the standard gains pro forma as usual (see Chapter 12).

The share pool

- Shares acquired before the disposal are pooled together in the share pool.

Share pool

	Number	Cost
		£
Purchase	X	X
Purchase	X	X
	X	X
Sale	(X)	(X) W1
Pool c/f	X	X

W1

$$\frac{\text{Number of shares sold}}{\text{Number of shares in pool}} \times \text{Cost to date}$$

Bonus issues

- A bonus issue = distribution of free shares to existing shareholders based on the number of shares owned.

- On a 1:4 bonus issue a shareholder with 400 shares would receive 100 free shares.

For capital gains purposes they are treated as follows:

- The bonus shares are not treated as a separate holding of shares.

- The shares are treated as acquired on the same day as the original shares to which they relate.

- Therefore, the number of bonus shares are included in the share pool but at nil cost.

Rights issues

- A rights issue = a distribution of shares, normally at less than market value, to existing shareholders based on the number of shares owned.

- On a 1:3 rights issue at £10 per share, a shareholder with 300 shares would acquire 100 shares at a cost of £1,000.

For capital gains purposes they are treated as follows:

- The rights shares are not treated as a separate holding of shares.

- The shares are treated as acquired on the same day as the original shares to which they relate.

- Therefore, rights shares are included in the share pool in the same way as a normal purchase.

Capital gains tax – private residence relief

- Private residence relief (PRR).

CBA focus

You need to be able to correctly calculate the amount of relief available on the disposal of a main private residence.

Private residence relief (PRR)

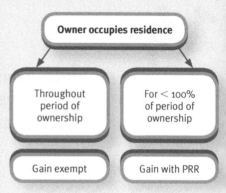

- Where there have been periods of absence by the owner calculate the gain as normal.
- Then calculate PRR.

Formula:

Exempt proportion of capital gain:

$$= \frac{\text{Periods of occupation (including deemed occupation)}}{\text{Total period of ownership}}$$

Key Point

PRR is given before deducting capital losses.

- Periods of occupation are periods of:
  - actual occupation, and
  - deemed occupation.

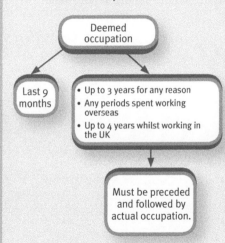

Deemed occupation

Last 9 months

- Up to 3 years for any reason
- Any periods spent working overseas
- Up to 4 years whilst working in the UK

Must be preceded and followed by actual occupation.

- An individual living in two properties can elect which one should be the PR.

15

Inheritance tax

- Charge to inheritance tax (IHT).
- Lifetime gifts.
- IHT computations.
- Diminution in value.
- Exemptions.
- Pro forma – Death estate.
- Residence NRB (RNRB).
- Married couples and civil partners.

CBA focus

Inheritance tax is tested in tasks 12 and 13 of the sample assessment.

Charge to inheritance tax (IHT)

- Occasions of charge:
    - Lifetime gifts
    - Death estate.
- Charged on:
    - a chargeable transfer (see later)
    - of chargeable property
    - by a chargeable person.
- Chargeable property:
    - all capital assets / wealth
    - no exempt assets for IHT.
- Chargeable person:
    - individuals domiciled in UK (on worldwide assets)
    - individual domiciled outside UK (on UK assets only).
- Gratuitous intent:
    - transfer must be a gift
    - intention to give asset away
    - not a poor business deal.

Lifetime gifts

- Three types:
  - Exempt (see later)
  - Potentially Exempt Transfers (PETs)
  - Chargeable Lifetime Transfers (CLTs).

	PETs	CLTs	
Definition	Gift by individual to another individual	Gift into a trust	
Chargeable	Only if donor dies within 7 years of gift	At date of gift	Additional IHT if donor dies within 7 years of gift
Tax rates	Death rates	Lifetime rates	Death rates
Tax paid by	Donee	Donee, or Donor (if so; gross up gift for tax paid)	Donee

IHT computations

An IHT charge can arise in 3 different situations. The computation in each situation is different and must be studied carefully.

(1) Lifetime transfers – IHT on CLTs.

(2) Death – additional IHT on PETs and CLTs.

(3) Death estate.

In each situation:

- Stage 1: Compute the chargeable transfer.
- Stage 2: Compute the taxable amount.
- Stage 3: Compute the tax.

Stage 1: The chargeable transfer

The first stage of the computation for each situation is always the same; compute the chargeable transfer:

	£	
Transfer of value:		
Value before	X	Diminution in
Value after	(X)	value principle
	—	
	X	
Deduct:		
Exemptions	(X)	See below
	—	
Chargeable transfer	A	

Order of exemptions:

(1) Small gifts, inter spouse and civil partner gifts, charities, political parties, museums and art galleries.

(2) Marriage exemption.

(3) AE – current year, then b/fwd.

Diminution in value

Gifts

- IHT uses the 'diminution in value' principle to calculate the 'transfer of value' (i.e. value by which the donor's estate has been reduced as a result of the gift).

	£
Value of estate before transfer	X
Value of estate after transfer	(X)
Transfer of value	X

- In most cases the transfer of value = value of asset gifted.

- In some cases the fall in value of the estate > value of the asset gifted (e.g. gift of unquoted shares).

Stage 2: Computing the taxable amount

Stage 2 is also the same for each situation. However, the calculation of the available nil rate band (NRB) differs.

	£
Chargeable transfer	A
Less:	
Available NRB	(X)
Taxable amount	X

Nil rate bands (NRB)

- For lifetime gifts – lifetime tax:
  - Use NRB in tax year of gift.
- For lifetime gifts – death tax:
  - Use NRB in tax year of death.
- For death estate:
  - Additional residence NRB available (see below).
  - Use NRB in tax year of death.

- The NRBs will be provided in the assessment where needed.

Stage 3: Computing the tax

1 – Lifetime tax on CLT (example – gift in 2017/18)

	£	£
Chargeable transfer		222,000
Less:		
NRB at gift (2017/18)	325,000	
Less: CLTs in 7 years prior to gift (say)	(183,000)	
NRB available		(142,000)
Taxable amount		80,000
IHT payable:		
(i) at 20% if donee pays tax		16,000
(ii) at 25% if donor pays tax		20,000

If donor pays tax:
Add IHT to value of chargeable transfer to calculate gross chargeable amount (£222,000 + £20,000) = £242,000.

Key Point

Note that the donor is primarily responsible for the lifetime tax due.

2 – Additional tax on lifetime transfers as a result of donor's death (example – death in 2020/21)

Gift – CLT or PET

	£	£
Gross chargeable transfer		365,000
Less:		
NRB at death	325,000	
Less: CLTs and chargeable PETs in 7 years prior to gift (say)	(140,000)	
NRB available		(185,000)
Taxable amount		180,000

	£
IHT payable at 40%	72,000
Less: Taper relief (40%)(say)	(28,800)
Chargeable (60%)	43,200
Less: Lifetime tax paid (say)	(10,000)
IHT payable	33,200

Taper relief

- Taper relief gives a percentage reduction in death tax liability

- Available if gift made over 3 years before death

- Higher percentage the longer period between gift and death

- The rates are provided in the assessment

Lifetime tax deduction

- Cannot create a repayment of IHT.

3 – IHT on death estate

Death estate computation:

	£	£
Value of Estate		925,000
Less:		
NRB at death	325,000	
Less: CLTs and chargeable PETs in 7 years prior to death (say)	(180,000)	
NRB available		(145,000)
Taxable amount		780,000
IHT payable at 40%		312,000

Exemptions

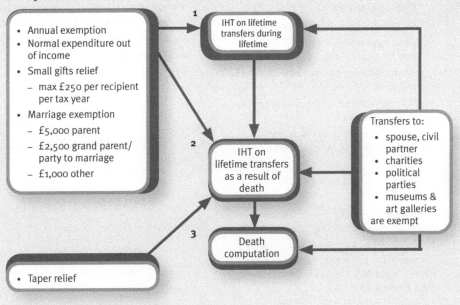

Annual exemption

- £3,000 per annum.
- Applied to gifts in chronological order.
- Used against PET – even if PET never becomes chargeable.
- Unused amount can be carried forward one year.
- Current year exemption used in priority to brought forward.
- Applied after all other reliefs and exemptions have been applied.

Normal expenditure out of income

- Gift is exempt if made as part of normal expenditure out of income (not capital).
- Must not effect donor's standard of living.
- Must be habitual.
- Level will depend on income of donor.

CBA focus

Exemptions are likely to feature in the assessment – it is important that you can identify when they are available and how they are applied.

Pro forma – Death estate

	£
Freehold property	x
Less: Mortgage	(x)
	x
Motor car	x
Life insurance proceeds	x
Cash and bank accounts (including ISAs)	x
All other assets owned by deceased	x
Debts due to deceased	x
	x
Less: Outstanding debts	(x)
Funeral expenses	(x)
	x
Less: Exempt legacies (note)	(x)
Chargeable estate	x
Inheritance tax payable	x

Paid by: Executors = personal representatives

Tax on death estate is usually suffered by:

- the residual legatee (i.e. recipient of 'the rest' of the death estate)
- not those receiving specific gifts.

Note: Exempt legacies are to spouse, civil partner, UK charities, political parties, museums and art galleries.

Key Point

All assets are chargeable
Exception: overseas assets owned by non-UK domiciled individual.

Assets that are exempt from CGT
(e.g. motor cars, gilts, ISAs, PPR, etc.)
are not exempt from IHT.

Residence NRB (RNRB)

The RNRB applies when:

- calculating the tax on the death estate (not on lifetime gifts)

- the death estate includes a residential property (that the deceased has lived in), and

- the property is inherited by the deceased's direct descendants (children or grandchildren).

The available RNRB = the lower of:

- £175,000

- the value of the property (net of any repayment mortgage).

The RNRB is applied before the normal NRB in the estate computation.

Married couples and civil partners

Transfer of unused NRB/RNRB

- If the NRB/RNRB has not been fully utilised at the time of a person's death, the unused proportion can be transferred to their spouse or civil partner.
- At their death, the surviving spouse or civil partner will have the benefit of:
  - their own NRB and RNRB, **and**
  - any unused percentage of their spouse's or civil partner's NRB and RNRB.

- The unused percentage is applied to the NRB/RNRB at the time of the surviving spouse or civil partner's death
  - **not** at the date of the first death.
- Where the spouse died before 6 April 2017 100% of the RNRB will always be available to transfer to the second spouse.

Index